FEELING GOOD

Please send for a free copy of the latest How To Books catalogue.
3 Newtec Place, Magdalen Road, Oxford OX4 1RE, United Kingdom
Or visit How To Books on-line at www.howtobooks.co.uk

FEELING GOOD

Proven tools
for lifelong happiness

Pete Cohen & Judith Verity

How To Books

Published by How To Books Ltd,
3 Newtec Place, Magdalen Road,
Oxford OX4 1RE. United Kingdom.
Tel: (01865) 793806. Fax: (01865) 248780
email: info@howtobooks.co.uk
http://www.howtobooks.co.uk

First published 1999
Reprinted and reformatted 2001

British Library Cataloguing in Publication Data.
A catalogue record for this book is available from the British Library.

Edited by Diana Brueton
Cover design by Baseline Arts Ltd, Oxford

Produced for How To Books by Deer Park Productions
Typeset and design by Baseline Arts Ltd, Oxford
Printed and bound in the United Kingdom

NOTE: The material contained in this book is set out in good faith for general
guidance and no liability can be accepted for loss or expense incurred as a result
of relying in particular circumstances on statements made in this book. Laws
and regulations are complex and liable to change, and readers should check the
current position with the relevant authorities before making personal
arrangements.

contents

about the authors

JUDITH VERITY

Judith Verity has worked in personal development for thirty years and has run her own training and counselling services. She joined Pete in writing for the highly successful *Lighten Up* slimming programme and is consulted regularly by the media on health and happiness issues.

PETE COHEN

Peter Cohen is a dynamic trainer and motivator who inspires and entertains his audiences. He started the *Lighten Up* programme ten years ago as an extension to his work as a personal trainer. He is a consultant on phobias and image problems and also appears regularly on television, including GMTV.

preface

This is a how-to-feel-better recipe book. You already have the ingredients, so you don't need to shop around for them. You can start getting it together straight away. Some ideas will work for you better than others, but you won't know which ones they are until you test them out.

Meanwhile we want you to read this book with an open and critical mind. We suggest you try out all the exercises and we recommend that you start writing your own Feelgood File. This is a life work by the way – but, as the shampoo commercial says, 'You're worth it'.

Pete Cohen & *Judith Verity*

I. feeling good

We either make ourselves miserable, or we make ourselves strong. The amount of work is the same.

Carlos Castaneda

IN THIS CHAPTER:

FEELING BAD

UNDERSTANDING CHEMICAL REACTIONS

FEELING GOOD

KNOWING HOW TO BE HAPPY

◆ Are you unhappy for no reason? Or unhappy for lots of reasons?

◆ Do you realise that it amounts to the same thing?

◆ Has bitter experience made you expect the worst, so at least when it happens – and it usually does – you're prepared?

◆ Are you reading this because you have the feeling that you've had enough and that it's time to feel less tired, less anxious and more optimistic?

AT THE BEGINNING OF EVERY CHAPTER we will suggest a goal that you might bear in mind as you read, and then review it again at the end of the chapter. **Setting yourself a challenge** every day or every week and **keeping a log of your progress** is one of the most dynamic tools of change. Writing down your thoughts and charting your progress gives you **focus and perspective** and you will surprise yourself with your **optimism and creativity**. So before you settle down to read, get yourself a notebook and pen. At the end of this book the notebook will be your own *Feelgood File*. Using a *Life Diary* as an instrument of personal change rather than a record for the archives is an inspiring habit to have. We expect that some of the *Feelgood Formulas* will be so effective that you will want to use them over and over again until you come up with your own personal ways and means to happiness.

FEELING BAD

Energy follows thought.
Julie Soskin

We all spend time imagining bad things that might happen. 'Expect the worst and hope for the best,' is the advice children are given. If that's what you were told – or what you tell your children – you might want to reconsider it. If the worst does happen, you'll cope a lot better if you haven't imagined not coping with it over and over again. You don't improve your disaster management mechanisms by doing that; you simply practise panicking.

So stop touching wood, throwing salt over your shoulder, avoiding black lines on the pavement and walking round ladders – or whatever it is that you do. Your personal bad luck charm may not be an obvious one, but it still amounts to looking for trouble.

Do these silly things matter? Of course. They are the tip of a very big iceberg of attitude that's under your surface. You think you're only paying lip service to the possibility of things going wrong? **You get what you focus on** – so when you constantly prepare for the worst, that's probably what you'll get.

Being disappointed, or lonely or irritated takes planning and preparation. So does having a good time – but we tend to leave that to chance.

Often our responses to everyday life tend to be negative rather than positive. We give negative commands all the time. What happens when you tell children not to spill the milk? It probably hadn't occurred to them before, but as soon as you say it, they think 'Spill the milk? Well, I suppose I might...' If you'd said, 'Carry the glass carefully,' or 'See if you can keep that milk level in the glass,' the outcome might have been different.

UNDERSTANDING CHEMICAL REACTIONS

Drugs don't make you happy –
but they take away the pain for a while.
Ginger Redbourn

The fastest way to blot out bad feelings is to adjust your chemical balance artificially. The quickest way to get temporarily happy is to use drugs.

These **external quick fixes** are very effective in the short term, regardless of whether the bad feelings result from boredom or overwork, from difficult relationships or from no relationships at all.

Unfortunately, the amount of relief we get from quick fixes is roughly in proportion to the negative side effects which follow. The bigger the buzz, the deeper the downside in terms of

◆ pain
◆ addiction
◆ and general malfunction.

We go out every day looking for pleasure and everybody can afford to buy it in small doses – a bar of chocolate, a beer, a cigarette, a prescription. But even the little, legal remedies for unhappiness can cause long term damage.

When is a bar of chocolate or a glass of wine as bad for your health as a line of cocaine? If you're taking something to **cover up feelings you can't cope with** rather than purely for pleasure, you're probably on the wrong track. It doesn't matter whether it's sex or popcorn – if you're using it just to ease the pain, it may have painful side effects. The only good reason for eating is hunger and the best sex isn't inspired by duty, insecurity, fear or finance.

◆ The solution to being unhappy is to be happy. Painkillers are only stopgap measures.
◆ The way to be happy is to generate your own internal happy chemicals.
◆ The recipes for those come later.

A lot of people have very **low expectations**. They don't expect to feel good, they just hope to feel better – or make their unhappiness bearable for a while. This is true even of hard drug users. The first few hits may be ecstasy, but in the end most addicts are taking their drug just to survive – the first blissful experience has long since gone. They are just getting by, like the rest of us, but they made the mistake of thinking there was an easy way out.

This isn't to say you should never take drugs. There are times when a cup of tea or a glass of wine has far more benefits than disadvantages. And sometimes a chemical imbalance needs a prescription to sort it out. But before you reach for the bottle or packet make sure you **weigh the benefits against the long term disadvantages**.

Think past the immediate relief to the long term result – what happens when the painkillers wear off? Will you feel as bad as you did before? Or worse?

You can sit down in front of the TV with a few beers and lose yourself in the latest crash and burn video. But when the movie's over you're left with your own negative feelings and probably a few extra as well – to say nothing of a hangover if you've really let yourself go for a good time.

♦ You may not notice your bad feelings for a while, but you've only swept them under the carpet.

♦ Sooner or later you're going to trip over the carpet and then you've got another problem to add to your collection.

Have you ever noticed that problems are like buses – they travel in convoys? You meet a person with a problem and often, as you get to know them better, you realise that they are a problem person. It's their way of life, how they define themselves, nothing to do with what actually happens to them.

FEELGOOD FORMULA
The Feelbad Scale

◆ Did you pick up this book because you just got tired of the way you feel?

◆ Or was it because life has become particularly hard to cope with just recently?

◆ How do other people see you? As a person with problems or a tower of strength that they can lean on? If you're not sure about the answer to this you might try asking some of your friends – but make sure you're prepared for whatever answer you get.

◆ If you divided up your day into a pie chart, what proportion of it would you spend feeling worried or depressed and what proportion not thinking about how you're feeling at all? Do you think the balance has changed much over the last five years?

Where would you put yourself on a scale which started at mildly dissatisfied and went right down to completely wretched?

The answers may pop straight into your head, or, you may need to sleep on it. Even if you get immediate answers, still sleep on it.

FEELING GOOD

You'll notice that we've asked you to define feeling bad before being asked to define feeling good – because for most people, it's a lot easier! However, **you get what you focus on**, so this book isn't about not feeling bad all the time, it's about **feeling good a lot more of the time**. What do you want to achieve?

♦ Do you just want to feel less anxious?

♦ Or do you think you could have a go at being truly, deeply happy?

Feeling good is bound to vary from one person to another – for some it's feelings of **comfort, safety and absence of fear**. For others it's **ecstasy, inspiration** and **feelings of omnipotence**. If it's a long time since you felt anything like happy, think about the last few days. Have there been the odd few seconds of happiness – or at least relief – when the sun shone unexpectedly, or you were caught unawares by a joke?

Now you know a little more about yourself, take a reality check on the rest of the world. How many people do you know who really feel good about themselves, value themselves and are contented? Include in this not only the people you know personally, but stars and celebrities too. They may be rich and famous with surgically enhanced bodies and beautiful homes, but are they happy? Allowing for the fact that the media usually highlights dysfunctional relationships and nervous breakdowns, are the 'It' girls and Rock Legends any nearer Nirvana than the rest of us? Probably they are about the same. They can *afford* to be addicted to dangerous substances and clock into exclusive clinics when they get depressed. But expensive remedies don't necessarily work much better than DIY ones, which is a good reason for reading this book.

◆ People who want to change and are ready to change will find a way to do it.

◆ If the key to happiness was in a bottle or on an operating table, the rich and famous would have bought their tickets to heaven and the tabloids wouldn't be writing about them any more.

So why is it that only a few people in life succeed in being happy? In fact, why do only a few people actually succeed at anything – whether it's business, sport or marriage? And how do they do it?

You don't feel happy because of what happens or happened to you. It doesn't matter why things go wrong or feel wrong.

What matters is how things feel wrong and how to change those feelings.

KNOWING HOW TO BE HAPPY

A happy person is not a person in a certain set of circumstances, but rather a person with a certain set of attitudes.
Hugh Downs

FEELGOOD FORMULA
The Feelgood File

◆ Get a notebook (your *Feelgood File*).

◆ Select some happy people you know. Choose people you know well.

◆ Watch how they do it. Better still, ask them. They may not know immediately, but they will probably work it out for you. Their feelings of happiness might not be identical to yours, but some of their methods will probably work for you.

◆ Write down the recipe in your *Feelgood File* and try it out for yourself.

There are formulas, strategies and techniques for feeling good. Our work with the *Lighten Up* programme has shown us that the easiest way to be slim is to copy what slim people do – and this principle can be applied to almost any skill you want to aquire.

Take cooking, for example. A great chef can produce a great meal with natural talent and years of training, but anyone can cook a good meal simply by following a good recipe. Your brain structure is physically the same as people who are much happier than you – everybody has the basic building blocks for happiness.

If you aren't happy, the chances are it's more to do with the way you are currently using your body and brain than with traumas lurking in your past.

□ □ □

Feelgood Factors

✔ If you plan for it and practise it, you can be good at feeling bad. But you have a choice.

✔ The way to be happy is to generate your own internal happy chemicals.

✔ Get your destination sorted out before you read on. Check out what feeling good really means for you and how much of it you think you can stand.

✔ There are formulas and recipes for feeling good. You can write them down in the *Feelgood File*, practise them and hard-wire them into your personal circuits.

2. using your brain for a change

Men are not prisoners of fate,
but only prisoners of their own minds.
Franklin D Roosevelt

IN THIS CHAPTER:

MIXING CHEMICAL COCKTAILS

USING THE POWER OF THOUGHT

GETTING WHAT YOU FOCUS ON

◆ Do you have the same worrying thoughts going round and round, day in and day out?

◆ Do you sometimes need distractions like television, constant company or alcohol, just because your mind is such an uncomfortable place to be alone?

◆ When people say 'Cheer up, it may never happen,' do you think to yourself, 'It usually does'?

SOME MORNINGS I GET UP AND I CAN'T DECIDE what to do first – in spite of having written what I thought was a definitive list the night before. I don't get days like that very often now – and when they do happen I have the tools to get sorted and started quite quickly.

But it wasn't always that way and I don't believe I was unusual. There are a lot of sensible adults who believe, fatalistically, that their brains have a mind of their own. 'My mind wandered,' we say, as if our whole psychological set-up could wilfully walk out on us. People are fatalistic about what's going on in their heads: 'I'll see what mood I'm in...' Take a good look at what sort of life you want and give yourself a good talking to.

The challenge for this chapter is to find out what being happy means to you. This is not an abstract definition of happiness we're aiming for but the feel, the smell, the taste and colour – and of course the sound – of happiness.

If you know what you want, you're more likely to get it.

MIXING CHEMICAL COCKTAILS

I believe happiness is inside all of us,
we just need to know how to turn it on.
Graham Sheargold, piano seller

The secret of feeling good more of the time and changing your mood at will is **learning to mix your own chemical cocktails**. The brain produces its own chemicals, including hallucinogens and endorphins. Some of them would be illegal if sold on the street and their effects range from bliss to psychosis. Did you know that with practice, you can gain control over the production process? You can learn to:

◆ selectively speed up production of the chemicals you want

◆ reduce, or disperse, the ones you don't.

This is, of course, slower than just buying the happy chemicals and washing them down with a glass of vodka, and it does take practice. On the other hand, it's safe and it's free. Plus, **results actually improve over the long term** – they don't decrease as your tolerance rises. And there's no liver damage.

How is it done? Remember the last time you felt really relaxed? Slipping into a warm bath perhaps, the water soothing and bathing you in relaxation from your toes to your nose. **As soon as you start thinking about a time when you were happy, your brain obligingly reproduces the feeling for you.**

You know you can do it. Everybody can. You're probably pretty good already at overproducing some of the uncomfortable substances you only need in emergencies (like adrenaline). You can learn to cut back on those fight or flight activators and increase the production of endorphins and serotonin at the touch of an imaginary button.

FEELGOOD FORMULA
Get Happy

The following exercise is a classic. It's one of many useful exercises which becomes more effective with practice. You can do it on the train, while you're walking the dog, or while you're sitting in a traffic jam. If you are doing it at home, get out your *Feelgood File* and capture some of the feelings.

◆ Find a quiet place and take a few moments to yourself. Sometimes being alone with time to think can be scary so we try to stay busy. Get used to being in a quiet space sometimes.

◆ Remember a time when you were happy. Even momentarily. It doesn't have to be a big deal. It could just be an unexpected win by your home team.

◆ Start in the present. Did you feel a flutter of happiness at the feel of the sun on your back today? A moment's moonlight on the river, a baby smiling, a face you love? See if you can collect up five or six of these from the past week and write them down.

◆ Go as far back as you like for a Feelgood memory and use that. Remember, you aren't looking for an extended period of bliss, just a moment of pure pleasure. And even when you're going through a bad patch, you can usually find a few seconds in a day when you forget to be unhappy.

◆ Remember each cheerful moment one at a time and check where in your body the happy feeling starts.

◆ When you've got something, run it through the standard checklist: What did you feel and where? A stomach flutter maybe? A glow around the heart? What did you see? What did you hear? What did you smell? Did taste come into it? You probably won't get all of these – unless you are exceptionally good at re-living experiences or you've done this exercise before.

If you can access a happy feeling, however briefly, what does that mean? It means that **your body and your brain know how to manufacture the chemicals that make you feel good.** And it's like riding a bicycle or driving a car. Once you've learned, you'll have that neural pathway built into your circuits. You may not have used it lately, but **you can find it again**, anytime.

FEELGOOD FORMULA
Find a Friend

If you prefer, you can do this with a friend to read out the questions and walk you through the experience. In fact it's a good idea to buddy with someone else for quite a few of the exercises in this book – or even get a group together. It's sometimes easier to stay motivated and focused through the early stages of something new when you're doing it with someone else.

USING THE POWER OF THOUGHT

Everything comes from thought – TV, chairs, toasters, aeroplanes. They all started as thoughts. The average person has about 50,000 thoughts in a day. In a 16-hour day that amounts to about four a second. Our minds are constantly whirring with ideas and impulses, plans and pictures.

Out of all those thoughts, how many of them are new? Are you constantly mulling over the same old ideas, beliefs, worries and fears? Every time you repeat a thought, you reinforce it, the circuit gets stronger and there's less room and less time for new, more creative ideas. If you aren't happy, **the first thing to change is your mind**.

Your thoughts control your life. Your thoughts are what you will become. Your thoughts are one of the strongest forces in the universe. With all this power at your command, wouldn't it be a good idea to **point your thoughts in the right direction** more often?

FEELGOOD FORMULA
The Brain Dump

You need your *Feelgood File* again for this.

◆ Over the next week, for 15 minutes a day, write down as many as possible of the things you think about.

◆ After a week your list will be a cross-section of what's on your mind: your fears, hopes, worries, expectations, people, places, memories and daydreams.

◆ Step back and take a critical look at what you've written. Does your thought inventory tell you that your mind is a nice place to live right now? Or is it stressful and depressing?

◆ If your thoughts aren't helping you, make a new list of the kind of thoughts you would like to have. Supportive thoughts, thoughts about yourself as a valuable, confident, healthy person.

Our minds are like heat-seeking missiles. If we focus them on what's wrong or missing in our lives, that's where they'll take us. If we think a lot about what frightens us, we are going to spend a lot of time feeling afraid. Make your new thought list positive and **start being curious about people you admire**, people who are good at being happy, relaxed or confident. Ask them how they do it and take notes.

FEELGOOD FORMULA
The Mission Statement

The power of thought is the secret that could change your life. If you let your thoughts run riot, then a riot is probably what you'll get. So stop it now and **take control**. Write your mission statement on a card and pin it up where you can see it – over your desk, on the bathroom mirror, on the dashboard of the car: **'My thoughts control my life'**.

FEELGOOD FORMULA
Mind-Changing

Pick up the *Feelgood File* again.

◆ Over the next few days, re-run the Brain Dump exercise.

◆ But this time, whenever you reach for the pen to write down a thought, evaluate it first. If it's positive, write it down.

◆ If it's a negative, worrying thought, edit it before you make a note. Make it positive, then write it down. For example: 'I hate this paintwork' could be 'I'll choose a nicer colour as soon as I get a break.'

GETTING WHAT YOU FOCUS ON

You'll see it when you believe it.
Wayne Dyer

If you spend your time crossing your fingers and running a damage limitation exercise on your life, you're probably maintaining the feel-bad status rather than alleviating it.

Successful people who feel good spend their time focused on what's positive and what's working rather than on the downside. If you worry constantly about things going wrong you are gearing up for a negative outcome. The chances are that if things did turn out well, you wouldn't believe it.

The way we feel is the direct result of what we think. We have thousands of thoughts every day and most of them are wasted. You have the power to hypnotise yourself into a position of powerlessness in just the same way that the big advertising companies do. Ask yourself 'what do beans mean?' and an answer will spring to mind – but beans don't really mean Heinz. If somebody else can do that to your brain in the interest of selling beans, think how much better you could do if you programmed it yourself.

A friend, whose kids had grown up wanted to move to a penthouse flat in the city. 'The trouble is, I can't do it because the boys' bedrooms are still full of their stuff and I feel like I'm rejecting them if I throw it out,' she said.

'Why don't you ask them to come over and sort it out?' I suggested.

Reluctantly she did, and three roomfuls of clutter were thrown out.

'Who's problem was it in the end?' I asked her.

'Mine, I suppose. I didn't really want to let them go – but I feel great now that I've done it. I'm ready to move on.'

Spring-clean your mind once in a while. Our minds fill up with our out-dated clutter – and sometimes they are littered with other people's old ideas. Check what's in your own memory bank and if it's getting you down, get rid of it. You may find thoughts and ideas that were useful once, but if they don't work for you any more, bin them.

You can set yourself up for success. Imagine a boxer looking at his opponent and thinking 'He looks big – I might get hurt.' Unlikely, isn't it?

When we think about our strengths, we are strong. When we think about our weaknesses, we are weak. If we tell ourselves things aren't going to work out, we're loading the dice the wrong way.

If we tell ourselves things are going to be fine we are already creating the internal resources we need to make things work.

Feelgood Factors

✔ You don't need to take drugs – you can manufacture your own. Since you are doing it anyway, you might as well take the trouble to get the prescription right.

✔ Once you realise you can produce your own anti-depressants, you can exercise your right to control your thoughts – rather than letting them control you.

✔ If you let your thoughts control you, they may not always take you in the right direction. If you want to feel better, start writing your own script.

3. Becoming Aware

We all live under the same sky,
but we don't all have the same horizon.
Konrad Adenauer

IN THIS CHAPTER:

INVESTIGATING PLEASURE AND PAIN

DISCOVERING AWARENESS

TRYING SOME DETECTIVE WORK

SOLVING THE PROBLEM

◆ Do you spend so much time trying to avoid disasters that you don't have time to actually do anything positive – let alone feel cheerful?

◆ Do you sometimes do something that backfires on you and say 'Why do I keep doing that?' then the next day you do it again?

◆ Can you always see where other people are messing up their lives – but your own problems are a mystery?

◆ Why is 'why?' the most common word used by people with problems?

HAVE YOU GOT A CLEAR IDEA of what happy feels like now? Take a look at your Feelgood File and run through the *Get Happy* exercise again if you're not sure.

This chapter is about pleasure and pain and how to tell the difference. If we asked you whether you knew the difference between what makes you happy and what hurts, you'd probably laugh. Ask yourself anyway – but you don't have to come up with an answer until you've run through the next few *Feelgood Formulas*.

The challenge for this chapter is to identify one of your dysfunctional behaviour patterns (anything from smoking to being late for work) and **find a functional alternative**. Even happy people have a few bad habits – and most people have lots! You can't change something you're unaware of and you can't make progress unless you know where you are going. **Awareness is the key** and there will be things you'll want to write down. So make sure you have your Feelgood File and pen beside you.

INVESTIGATING PLEASURE AND PAIN

The first thing a physician must learn is to tell the difference between the disease and the battle of the body to protect itself. He will need a cure for the first and balm for the second. If he should confuse them, the patient may die.

Brother Aelred

The need to avoid pain is biological. It's built into our nervous system. Physically we protect ourselves without even thinking about it. When you put your hand on something hot, you don't keep it there. It's a pity our psychological protection systems aren't as efficient. In fact they can be downright dysfunctional. When we feel unhappy, do we react immediately and move away from the source of the pain? No. We're much more likely to intensify the problem by adding another piece of negative behaviour, like getting drunk when we feel lonely or overworking because we feel insecure. It doesn't resolve the issue, it just distracts us temporarily and leaves us with more problems to deal with in the long run. It's like leaving your hand on the stove and taking morphine to kill the pain. You could end up being a drug addict with third-degree burns.

This book is not about how to cope with feeling bad. It's about feeling good.

DISCOVERING AWARENESS

The better I get, the more
I realise how much better I can get.
Martina Navratilova

There's a story about awareness that appears in many books of philosophy and spiritual advice. This is the simpler version by Philip Kapleau.

One day a man of the people said to Zen Master Ikkyu: 'Master, will you please write for me some maxims of the highest wisdom?' Ikkyu immediately took his brush and wrote the word 'Attention.'

'Is that all?' asked the man. 'Will you not add something more?'

Ikkyu then wrote twice running: 'Attention, Attention.'

'Well,' remarked the man rather irritably, 'I really don't see much depth or subtlety in what you have just written.'

Then Ikkyu wrote the same word three times running: 'Attention, Attention, Attention.'

Half-angered, the man demanded: 'What does that word "attention" mean anyway?'

And Ikkyu answered gently: 'Attention means attention.'

TRYING SOME DETECTIVE WORK

*Real difficulties can be overcome. It is only the
imaginary ones that are unconquerable.*
Theodore N. Vail

A friend of mine thought his wife was cheating on him. I
met him in the pub one night and he told me he had hired
a private detective to follow her and see if she was having
an affair. 'What's the point?' I asked him.

'I have to know what's going on,' he said, 'then I can
see if there's a chance of saving the marriage. I still love her.'

'In that case, why don't you call up the detective and
asked him to follow you instead?' I suggested. 'You've got
more chance of saving the marriage if you take a look at
your own behaviour and find out what you're doing that
might have driven her away – or made you paranoid –
whichever it turns out to be.'

Find out what's causing the problem. As a sign in
a bar says, 'The past is the past and the future's not here
yet. This moment, right now, is a gift. That's why it's called
the present.'

We're not talking about digging around in the traumas
of your early childhood here. The past can be a distraction,
a justification or a smokescreen – whatever you want it to
be. When you're going through a period of unhappiness, the
first thing to do is **bring into conscious awareness** all the

automatic things you do every day. Everything we do causes pain or pleasure – so why don't we just stop doing the stuff that causes us pain and get on with being happy? If only it was that simple.

We worked with a lady who was worried about her weight – she had been dieting and exercising unsuccessfully for 12 years. At her office there was a gymnasium for the staff – in a beautiful penthouse suite on the 20th floor. After work one day she was stressed and irritable. 'Even when I do try to keep fit,' she said, 'everything goes against me. I was booked for a session with my trainer today and then the lift broke.'

'Why didn't you just walk up the stairs?' we asked her.

'Don't be silly, I'd be too tired to do my workout.'

Now this lady would go out for dinner claiming not to have eaten all day because she really was unaware of the constant biscuits and sweet tea and coffee she was drinking. She was shocked when we got her to write down how much and how often she was eating between meals. And even more surprised when she realised that she was standing still on escalators and worrying about being a couple of minutes late for work. After all, if she was late for work she'd feel guilty about taking a full lunch break to go to a step class.

◆ There are lots of things we all do every day that make us unhappy and we don't even notice them.

◆ They might be things we started doing for a good reason – but we carried right on doing them, long after the reason was gone.

Take smoking for example. Children start smoking because it seems like a good idea at the time – they want to look sophisticated, they want to annoy their parents or they want to be like their friends. After a while they can't break the habit and eventually they become 30-somethings spending a fortune on hypnosis and nicotine patches because they're so desperate to quit.

SOLVING THE PROBLEM

There was an old lady who swallowed a fly, I don't know why, she swallowed a fly, perhaps she'll die.
There was an old lady who swallowed a spider, that wriggled and tickled and tickled inside her, she swallowed the spider to catch the fly...

Everybody knows the end of that story – she was killed by the remedy for a non-life threatening problem.

So why not ruthlessly **abandon all the painkiller activities** we mentioned in Chapter 1, things which make you temporarily happier (or just mask the pain) but eventually leave you in a worse state than before. Then **strip out the behaviour patterns or feelings** that the painkillers were installed to cover up but didn't. Wouldn't that leave you with just the things that make you happy?

In fact, why haven't you done that already? Probably because, if you're like most people, **you don't actually know what's making you happy and what's making you depressed**.

FEELGOOD FORMULA
The Hidden Agenda

There are lots of drugs and activities and behaviour patterns that work like that. If we were more aware of what they were doing to us – and what they *weren't* doing *for* us – we'd have more chance of giving them up. If you know *why* you're doing something that makes you unhappy, you've got the option to satisfy that need some other way.

◆ Select one of your own behaviour patterns that you'd like to change. Don't go for a big problem to start with – start with something small, like the half-hour you waste watching something pointless on TV and then going to bed feeling vaguely dissatisfied.

◆ Ask yourself, 'Am I getting any benefits from this behaviour – even though it makes me feel bad in the long run? And just what might those benefits be?'

◆ If the answer is that you're avoiding something unpleasant such as boredom, insomnia, or the washing up, tackle the real issue. Call a friend, do a mini-workout, walk the dog – or even do the washing up and treat yourself to a clean kitchen in the morning. You'll soon find that three and a half hours of unwanted viewing per week quickly disappears.

Get into the habit of **running this check regularly** on any habits that aren't comfortable, whether it's overeating, drinking, sleeping too much, sleeping too little, under-exercising, over-exercising, destructive relationships, no relationships or job dissatisfaction. Anything in fact that you regularly do which gets you down or lets you down.

Everything we do serves a purpose. And watching half an hour of TV will certainly put off the washing up, put you to sleep or put boredom in perspective. But if you end up going to bed every night in a bad mood because of it, then there's an easy answer: **find another way of satisfying those needs**, one that doesn't have side effects.

You are likely to get negative side effects if you do things for negative reasons.

Playing solitaire for an hour because you can't face writing a report is bound to leave you jaded. If you got up from your desk and did something that needed doing anyway – like shopping, cooking, meditating, watering the garden – you would probably feel more energised when you finally sat down in front of your screen again.

Feelgood Factors

◆ Are you trying to numb the psychological pain rather than identifying and removing the cause?

◆ The first step to being happy is to become aware of what's making you unhappy and get rid of it. Once you know what you're doing, you can find some other way of meeting the need.

◆ Awareness of your own behaviour is what matters. You can't change anyone's behaviour but your own and you can't change a relationship unless you change your own role in it first.

◆ Before you rush in to eliminate a behaviour pattern or solve a problem, check that:
— the problem is really the problem
— you take out not just the problem itself but also any harmful or unnecessary painkillers and subsidiary behaviour patterns that have grown out of it.

4. getting in a Right state

*I discovered I always have choices and
sometimes it's only a choice of attitudes.*
Judith Knowlton

IN THIS CHAPTER:

AVOIDING DEATH AND DESTRUCTION

BEING STRONG ENOUGH TO SURVIVE

GETTING IN A RIGHT STATE

◆ Have you ever wondered why it's so much easier to feel
bad than to feel good? Why it's so much easier to churn
out adrenaline than endorphins?

◆ Are you better at getting into a right old state than
getting into the right state? Why is it that one seems to
come more naturally than the other?

A MAN ON ONE OF OUR *LIGHTEN UP* COURSES injured his back and could hardly move for a week. He asked his GP whether he needed an X-ray. The GP said, 'If I sent every single one of my patients for an X-ray, it would probably show a spinal lesion somewhere that might account for some pain. I've come to the conclusion that some people just sit, stand and walk more efficiently than others.'

It's the same with feeling bad. Most of us can dig up a childhood trauma that would account for quite a bit of misery. But some of us are miserable and some aren't...so **could happiness have more to do with how we live our lives than with what happens to us?** If that's true, then the key to being in a better state to cope with life must be **the action we choose to take**. We can be responsible for our own lives and our own happiness. This chapter's challenge is to start using your *Feelgood File* as a time-saving, stress-saving, state-changing tool. Give it time to see how well it could work for you in the much, much longer term.

AVOIDING DEATH AND DESTRUCTION

Cry havoc and let slip the dogs of war.
Shakespeare – Julius Caesar

We do seem perversely attracted to disasters. Some of the most thrilling stories and the most quotable quotes are violent and stirring. Why is death and destruction so enjoyable and what can we do about it? Most of us like talking to our friends, we're social animals, but what do we talk about? Do we tell each other how well we're feeling and how many wonderful things our colleagues have done for us in the last week? Isn't the conversation more likely to be about our latest health scare, how someone let us down, the car wouldn't start and it rained every day at the weekend?

And what about other forms of recreation? The cinema for example. Most box office hits have a high murder and mayhem content. It seems that the more sedentary our lifestyle and the more sterile our environment, the more excitement we need.

People are designed to live with danger and conflict – the suicide rate goes down during periods of war. But our coping mechanisms are fight or flight – and either way, that means active physical participation.

We were never meant to be passive observers so if we watch too many death and destruction movies, we internalise the violence and then wonder why we don't feel cheerful when we go about our daily business.

The same trend is apparent on the home front. Families are fragmented these days and people often live alone or in one parent families. Soap operas can be a substitute for large extended families, but they're dangerous because they don't provide a balanced range of emotions or any personal support.

In companies where employees feel powerless and don't have much control over what they do, there is usually a lot of absenteeism. And if we have a high, regular intake of fear and excitement but don't actually play a part in it, there is a steady build-up of anxiety which eventually turns into depression.

The brain produces chemicals to deal with stressful situations. It produces them just the same, whether we're actually dealing with a tough situation or sitting in a darkened cinema watching a bunch of men shooting at each other or a couple arguing on-screen. In terms of feelings, we can't tell the difference between the scenes we watch and the scenes we take part in. But there is a difference. The difference is that **we can only resolve emotional issues by getting involved and dealing with the crisis.** If we simply sit and watch, tension builds up. Then we wonder why we can't sleep.

BEING STRONG ENOUGH TO SURVIVE

At last, I think I've discovered the secret.
Do what you want to do, but do it.
Truman X Jones

FEELGOOD FORMULA
Being a Contender

♦ **Reduce your exposure to media stress.** You don't have to stop listening to the news, though you might stop watching it and reading the more sensational versions. Review your viewing and reading habits and ask yourself if you are letting too much unhappiness and violence (disguised as information or entertainment), into your life.

♦ **Find an emotional outlet that you can participate in, rather than just watching.** We're not advocating another war as an emotional and physical outlet for the current generation of young men and women, or more football violence (which seems to meet the same needs). Usually some regular, intensive (but comfortable) physical exercise defuses the tension just as effectively. There are plenty of martial arts classes and competitive contact sports on offer. Try Tai Chi or Chi Kung or one of the other oriental disciplines that focuses and channels energy. Experiment until you find the form that suits you.

◆ **Get involved.** If your life is seriously short of emotional participation, go out and join something. Get a job or volunteer to work in a charity shop, take a further education class in car mechanics or mediaeval art, anything that involves talking to real people – and arguing with them if necessary. If face-to-face seems a bit threatening you could start with the internet and gradually move your PC towards the door until going out seems like the logical next step. Interacting with real people at your local community or theatre group may not be as steamy and glamorous as watching East Enders, but it will feel much more satisfying.

When you become an active participant in life, rather than a helpless spectator, you gain strength. **Exercise for the mind is as good as exercise for the body.** You have to make a bit of an effort, especially at the beginning of any lifestyle change, but being depressed and having low self esteem also takes skill and application – and being depressed is much more tiring than being cheerful.

GETTING IN A RIGHT STATE

Learn to be intense without being tense.
Pressure is not tension.
Joe Torre

Whatever you do, whatever you are feeling – good or bad – requires effort from you. Being anxious, bad tempered or sad is not like being struck by lightning or illness or a bus. You may have been miserable for so long that you aren't aware of participating in the process, you may even think that it's just something that happens to you. But don't be fooled. You've simply become so good at having low self esteem that your subconscious is handling all the necessary procedures without even asking your permission.

◆ The first step is to become aware of the subconscious processes you may be running. Not *why* you're doing things but *what* you're doing.

◆ The second step is to look at your state of mind and experiment with ways of changing, at will, from a negative state to a positive one. And that is as easy as it sounds.

We actually think in pictures. If asked what you were doing half an hour ago, certain images would come to mind. When we become depressed, anxious or worried, we picture certain things that make us feel that way. If you think of your mind as a picture gallery where you are the curator and can change the exhibition at will, you begin to see that you can control what's going on in there.

◆ Have you ever had the feeling that everything is going right – at a meeting, playing a game, falling in love?

◆ Or the opposite feeling – the sort you get in one of those dreams that seems to go on for ever – you're late, you can't find your car keys, you're wearing the wrong clothes, you haven't got the information you need, you don't have a map, but you do have a killer hangover. These are the days when there's likely to be a traffic jam, derailed trains, electricity failure and a burst water main so you can't even have a shower.

On days like these, in spite of all the evidence to the contrary **you're the same person and the world's the same place**.

So why do you get different results at different times? There are great examples of this in sport – every athlete has experienced glory and defeat in the same week. And everybody knows that it's not a matter of talent, wealth or opportunity.

◆ How many people do you know who have academic qualifications and can't seem to keep a job?

◆ How many beautiful women and men in dysfunctional relationships?

◆ How many people born with a silver spoon who feel worthless?

Being in a good state is nothing to do with wealth, talent or opportunity. If you feel worried, anxious, sad or lonely you're just in a bad state. So how can you change it?

Imagine one of those parallel universe scenarios, like the film *Sliding Doors*. You're due at a meeting and the timing goes wrong. The phone rings as you are leaving, you can't find your notes, the car battery's dead. Fifteen minutes after the meeting was due to start, you are still in a traffic jam. Your phone rings and you just know that it's a call from the office wanting to know where you are. But the phone's in your bag on the back seat and you can't reach it. You picture the people who are waiting for you, impatient and annoyed. Stress starts in the pit of your stomach and spreads. Your heart rate and your breathing are getting faster as your blood pressure rises. The adrenaline you are generating creates scary pictures of what might happen. The meeting might be over before you even get there, then you'll be in trouble, maybe even out of a job.

By the time you *do* arrive you are harassed and sweating and even if they've waited for you and nobody is upset, you feel terrible. You're edgy and unfocused and give a poor performance.

Maybe you've put your job at risk. You've certainly put your health on the line. Like many other useful substances, adrenaline is functional in small doses and toxic in large ones. It doesn't take much human adrenaline to kill a guinea pig, and too much of it is very bad for human beings as well.

Alternatively ... just suppose that instead of panicking when you thought you were late, you had handled the situation differently?

◆ As soon as you realised you were working yourself up into a state, you'd have tackled that first and then informed the other people involved.

◆ When you got that uncomfortable feeling in your chest, a voice in your head might have said soothingly: 'OK, it looks like I'll be late. My best plan right now is to stay calm and positive. This meeting is important and I'm going to have to get my point across in less time than I'd planned.'

◆ This message is translated into your body and you adjust your breathing drawing a few long, deep breaths down into your stomach and you concentrate on letting out the air slowly.

◆ You take an extra couple of moments and pull into the side of the road to phone the office about the delay . You talk through some of the issues with a couple of people who won't be able to wait for you and the others get on with something else and re-schedule to meet you later.

Panicky people are late people – their time management is poor because they waste time worrying instead of preparing. They run round in circles looking for things they've lost. There's nothing glamorous about living that way – so **take some pressure off yourself by being very boring and getting organised**. It's cheaper than therapy and sometimes the results are surprisingly pleasant.

☐ ☐ ☐

FEELGOOD FORMULA
Being Boring

If I spent as much time doing the things I worry about getting done as I do worrying about doing them, I wouldn't have anything to worry about.
Beryl Pfizer

◆ In your *Feelgood File*, make a commitment now to spend time every day on getting your life organised so you don't waste time on the small stuff. Make a separate commitment to spend the same amount of daily time on yourself and your feelings. Give these two items equal billing.

◆ In your *Feelgood File* draw two pie charts with 24 or 48 slices to represent a 24-hour cycle.

◆ Fill in one the way you think you spend your time, and the other the way you would like to spend your time. Allow time for every part of your life: work, exercise, social interaction, personal development, sleep, family time – whatever is important to you.

◆ Include two essential categories:
1. Self management time
2. Self assessment time.

◆ Over the next three weeks, fill in one pie every day with the way you *really* spend your time.

◆ At the end of the three weeks, review your charts. Compare them with your original ones.

◆ Make a decision to change at least one of the activities. Maybe less working and more playing the piano; or more working and less time in the pub. Whatever you think might make a difference.

◆ After a week, review it again and get into the habit of:
1. Weekly reviews (same day and time every week)
2. Conscious adjustment of the various categories to see which ones make a difference to your happiness.

◆ Even if the *Being Boring Formula* is a bit picky for you, do it anyway. Then you can make yourself feel better instantly with the *Magic Circle*.

FEELGOOD FORMULA
The Magic Circle

◆ Imagine a circle in front of you on the floor. Step into it and repeat the *Get Happy* formula from Chapter 2. Imagine that in that circle is one of the greatest experiences you ever had in your life. One when you were happy, confident and strong. Notice what happens to you when you feel so good. Step inside that feeling like trying on a new suit or a new skin. Re-live that experience, make it bigger brighter and louder. Then step back out of the circle, leaving the experience right there inside it.

◆ Repeat this three times. When you've finished, you may find that just stepping inside the circle is enough to trigger those feelings of comfort and security and the warm glow of positive happiness.

◆ Do this exercise every day. To begin with you might like to designate a particular area in your house or garden for this. Some people use a rug, or a particular terrace area marked off by plants. I have a friend who tiled his own conservatory floor with a circle pattern built into the design – his *Magic Circle*. He doesn't tell most people what it's for.

Feelgood Factors

✔ Once you have taken the decision to reorganise what's going on inside your head, you might as well start on what's happening outside as well. It's no use sweeping the rubbish out of the back door if the front door's open, you'll just get more rubbish blowing right in off the street.

✔ Stand up and fight – observers in any situation are always in worse shape than participants.

✔ You control your state of mind. If you can feel bad – which takes effort and preparation – you can feel good – which takes less effort and preparation but more confidence.

5. coming to your senses

However much they offer you,
never work with a weak script.
Hedera Foley

IN THIS CHAPTER:

COMING TO YOUR SENSES

CASTING

SEEING THE FUTURE

CHANGING THE SOUNDTRACK

♦ Is your life a glorious technicolor production with a wonderful soundtrack? Or a black and white arthouse movie? A horror film? Are you the star – or just a bit player?

♦ Do you wake up in the morning knowing which scene you want to shoot and who's going to be playing opposite you?

◆ Or do you more often feel like the tea lady, the make-up artist, or the gopher?

◆ Are you dependent on the whim of the director – or are you in charge of creating the magic and making it happen?

WE PAY LIP SERVICE TO FREE WILL and self-determination but often live our lives as if our fate was written in the stars —or dictated by some arrogant film director with only the box office in mind. We behave as if we are powerless – and feeling powerless leads to lack of energy, low self-image and despair.

But it's only a feeling. The truth is that we experience the world through our **senses** – which are within our own control. We can use our senses **to create any future we want**.

Imagine you're making a film of your life – and the best bits are still to come. You can have any script and any ending you like, you choose the supporting cast, props, location and publicity machine. You are your own producer, designer and soundtrack composer as well as playing the leading role. The best technology – your own senses – is at your fingertips. You are ready to make the movie of your dreams.

COMING TO YOUR SENSES

You get the world through your senses. Sight, sound, smell, touch and taste are all that most of us have. And even when there's no external input, we experience our inner feelings in just the same way. When we're asleep, we dream in colour, people speak, music plays and all our other senses are there too.

Most of us have access to a broad range of sensory input and output, but most of the time we just let it happen. We don't use it to make ourselves feel better. In fact, if we use it at all it's usually to make ourselves feel worse.

A colleague of mine went through a phase of worrying about her husband and children coming home late. She started worrying about them half an hour before they were due, and gradually she became more and more anxious until she was worrying two hours in advance. Eventually she started worrying almost as soon as they left the house in the morning.

'How do you worry about them?' I asked her. 'What makes you feel bad when you think about them being late?'

'Well, it would just be so awful if anything happened to them. What would I do?'

'You'd probably cope.' I said. She was a woman who always coped in a crisis but just imagining a crisis made her picture herself *not* coping and then she felt bad.

A week after that conversation, I met her by the coffee machine at work. It was first thing in the morning and she was already looking stressed. When she got her coffee I persuaded her to sit down with me for a few minutes.

'I'm just an anxious person,' she said.

'There's no such thing as an anxious person,' I told her. 'You're just doing a lot of anxiety at the moment. What do you do that makes you feel bad? And how do you do it?'

When we talked it through, it was clear that she was seeing a picture which upset her. As soon as she thought about her family being late, she would visualise what might happen. This was usually a road accident, which she saw in graphic detail right down to the ambulance arriving and the scene in the A&E department. She had worked as an A&E receptionist before joining us, so she could reproduce this in lots of gory detail.

Once we had worked out together what was actually going on, we were able to change the anxiety process. Obviously the picture had to go. We didn't get rid of it altogether, not immediately. First I got her to make it smaller, darker, further away. I got her to remove herself from it so that she was looking at it from the outside rather than playing a starring role. She shrunk it to the size of a snapshot we could put in a drawer with a lot of other photos of her family doing boring things. Stuck in traffic jams, standing at bus stops and held up with computer problems at work. The scary one was lost amongst the others – and if she pulled it out by mistake she just mentally shuffled it to the back of the pile.

FEELGOOD FORMULA
The Problem Zapper

Did you ever get together with a group of other people to practise some of the *Feelgood Formulas*? The Problem Zapper is one that works really well if someone else talks you through it for the first few goes.

◆ If something is bothering you: check which of your senses is letting that problem in. Are there scary pictures? Is there an internal voice whining at you? Are you getting hot, faint and shaky when you're under pressure?

◆ Don't try not to think about it. Play around with it a little until you prove to yourself that everything coming into your mind is ultimately under your control.

◆ Make the pictures smaller, further away, fuzzy, give them silly frames, send them on a rocket to the moon. If a voice is saying 'you screwed up again', or 'she thinks you're boring' – change the tonality. Make it a Mickey Mouse voice, a Greta Garbo voice. Anything that turns you on or, better still, makes you laugh.

◆ Most important – detach yourself from the pictures or voices or feelings. If you're hot and trembling with fear, picture yourself on the other side of the room, standing under a cool shower.

Get away from it all. This sense of detachment, dissociation, or distancing is one of the greatest gifts you can give yourself. Have you ever listened to a friend talking about something that worried them and afterwards, you've said to yourself 'He's just got it all out of proportion. He needs a sense of perspective. He needs to get away.'

Have you ever fished a weeping girlfriend out of the toilet at a party when her date has taken someone else home and said: 'It will look different in the morning.' A cliché perhaps, but all clichés have that grain of truth that can be as powerful as a grain of the right drug in the right circumstances.

If something scares you – move away from it. Or move it away from you.

If you are in the habit of imagining yourself being fired or rejected or failing in any situation, the first step is to look at that picture from the outside – stay out of that picture – don't step into the frame.

FEELGOOD FORMULA
Association Change

◆ Get together with your *Feelgood File*, and your group – if you have one.

◆ Take a ho-hum experience: your journey to work, opening your front door, washing up, driving to the supermarket...

◆ Run through the activity. How do you see it? Are you looking at the experience from the outside – as if you were behind a camera filming it? Or are you right there *in* it, looking out through your own eyes as it happens?

◆ Try something else, this time with a little more positive emotional charge to it – one of your *Get Happy* experiences perhaps.

◆ Make exactly the same observations. Are you inside, living the experience, playing the starring role, or are you watching it from behind the camera?

◆ Take yet another experience, this time something negative but not too traumatic. Sitting an exam, getting up on Monday morning after a late Sunday night...

◆   Where are you this time? Are you inside the experience? Or filming it from the outside?

This exercise will tell you quite a lot about how you treat your experiences.

The key to personal success is to be FLEXIBLE. The more behaviour options you have the greater your chance of being happy regardless of your circumstances.

Wouldn't it be great if you could **choose how to experience the real and imaginary events of your life?** When you're late for work, when you're sitting in the dentist's chair, when you're in a difficult interview – wouldn't those be good times to step out of the experience and be a dispassionate observer?

What about other situations – being with someone you love, sharing a wonderful meal, winning a prize? Wouldn't it be a pity if you were detached and remote on those occasions? Happy people typically have the knack of **getting right into their good experiences and distancing themselves from the unpleasant ones.** Not surprisingly, unhappy people tend to do the opposite.

◆   What do you do?

◆   And if you aren't happy, are you ready to change?

FEELGOOD FORMULA
Editing your experiences

This is the time to take seriously your dual role of director and star of your personal movie. Know when to step back and detach yourself – edit out the scary bits completely if you want to – but at least make sure you aren't right there in the middle of them.

Then, when it's time for the big love scene – or whatever turns you on – make sure you're right there getting the benefit of every bit of it. This is the time when **extra sensory perception** takes on a whole new meaning. Let somebody else take over the directing and the camera.

CASTING

Le mariage – c'est un duet ou un duel.
French saying

That's true of most relationships. But **you can control the nature and quality of your relationships.** Take a look at your co-stars. If you always pick people who bore you or abuse you or neglect you or disrespect you, then fire them and hire somebody else. **It's your life.** OK, you can't get rid of your parents or your children, but just about every other relationship in your life is optional.

◆ You may be the victim in an abusive partnership – remember that it's not any more healthy for your abuser than it is for you – you're doing them a favour by telling them to walk.

◆ If you are surrounded by lacklustre individuals who seem to value you mainly for your selfless willingness to listen to their troubles, maybe you've been indulging them for too long. Give yourself and them a break.

◆ If you lie down and look like a doormat, you'll probably be walked on.

◆ If you're frequently aggressive, you're unlikely to be loved and respected.

Your own behaviour determines how others treat you – although there may also be people in your life who have their own reasons for needing you to be depressed, anxious, dependent or even aggressive and overbearing.

Once you have positive, encouraging voices in your head and a clear vision of who you are and where you want to be, you are already in a much stronger position for coping with the demands of others. **Unless you meet your own basic needs first, you can't engage in constructive relationships with anyone else.**

Consciously select more nurturing, loving, life-giving relationships. You are not duty bound to hang out with whingers and whiners – if you do, you might turn into one yourself.

SEEING THE FUTURE

Dreams aren't a matter of chance but a matter of choice.
David Copperfield

If we were to tell you to deliberately spend ten minutes every day envisaging yourself being very ill you'd quite rightly refuse to do it. Most people know that's a bad idea – yet those same people may spend time every day worrying about their health. Lots of people accept that being depressed or traumatised can make them physically ill but they wouldn't consider spending ten minutes every day envisaging themselves being fit and healthy.

□ □ □

FEELGOOD FORMULA
The Dress Rehearsal

Don't wait for the last take of the day to get it right. If there's something you want, whatever it is, rehearse, rehearse, rehearse. Make it so that your mind can't imagine any other future for you than the one you've practised.

◆ Choose what you want and give it the first read through. Do you want to be thinner? Do you want a better job? Do you want to be fitter and healthier? Do you want a more active social life?

◆ Imagine yourself walking towards your front door. Get right into yourself. You're the star this time, see it through your own eyes, not through the neighbour's window.

◆ Step up to the door and open it.

◆ In the hallway you can see yourself in that future you've been thinking about. See how wonderful you look. What you're wearing. The expression on your face. The difference in your skin, your muscle tone and your energy.

◆ Make that 'you' brighter, bolder, stronger, louder, clearer and larger than life.

◆ In anticipation of that new 'you' fully connect to it and feel how good it feels.

◆ Step into that future 'you' and become a part of the new scenario.

◆ Repeat this – often – until your desired future starts to feel very real indeed. Each time feel it stronger than you did before, turning up the sound and volume until there is no room for anything else in your head.

CHANGING THE SOUNDTRACK

Home, home on the range, where the deer and the antelope play, where never is heard a discouraging word, and the skies are not cloudy all day.

We talk to ourselves all the time. Unhappy people constantly make negative remarks. It's quite normal for a sane person to have several different voices in their head at the same time going 'You screwed up again', 'Whatever do you look like?', 'This isn't going to work', 'When will you ever learn', 'She's not going to like you'...

You may not be consciously aware of them, but they are certainly affecting your mood and behaviour. Spend today noticing what you say to yourself. It may be a constant niggle, an intermittent blast of condemnation, a drone of discouragement or a headache-level roar.

◆ Make a conscious choice to install a more encouraging sound track. You can change the words, the tone, the pitch and the position of the speakers or add music, if you want to.

◆ You can also change the content of the dialogue inside your head, you can adopt the specific postures or breathing patterns that go with different states that you'd like to be in. Simple.

Think of it as managing your internal communication. Or directing your own film. The sound track, the special effects and lighting are all at your command. You can direct your mental activity, with the skill and power of Steven Spielberg on a movie set.

Feeling good is no accident. There are clear differences between people who feel good all the time and people for whom feeling really good is so rare that they hardly recognise it when it happens.

Feelgood Factors

✔ Your senses are much more than a window on the world. They are the tools you can use to script and rehearse your own future. They belong to you, you don't belong to them – you can control the volume and intensity of all your experiences. All you need to do is locate the volume button and the on/off switch and learn to use them.

✔ It's your life. Pick talented people you can work with creatively, or at least pick loveable ones who value you.

✔ Visualisation is one of the most powerful self help tools you can use, but like all powerful tools it can be dangerous. Nightmares are simply visualisations which spring from fear and negativity rather than love and optimism.

✔ If you must talk to yourself at least say nice things. If you can't be nice, be quiet.

6. Getting out of your box

I have accepted fear as part of life – specifically the fear of change. I have gone ahead in spite of the pounding in the heart that says: turn back.

Erica Jong

IN THIS CHAPTER:

GETTING OUT OF YOUR HEAD

GETTING INTO YOUR BODY

RESPECTING YOURSELF

GETTING OUT OF YOUR BOX

♦ Do you have days when you feel as though you're in slow motion, nights when you can't sleep but you can't get up and do anything either, mornings when you don't want to get out of bed?

♦ Do you sometimes feel down and wonder when things will start looking up?

♦ If the same old thing is getting you down, it's time to make a change.

DID YOU THINK THIS BOOK was about living more comfortably? No, **comfort is for cats and you are a human being**. You were designed for risk and adventure, not for a comfortable life. Some of the great mystics of the millennium have recognised that **peace is to be found in chaos**.

Unless you face the things that scare you, they will eventually consume your life. It's like dieting. You want to lose a few pounds so you go on a diet. Soon you're spending a lot of time every day thinking about food, about what you can't eat and desperately want to eat.

The challenge for this chapter and the rest of your life is to **purposefully set about the task of feeling good**. Don't wait until you get that new job or new relationship or new baby or lots of money. It's up to you from now on to keep your *Feelgood File* going and personalise it so that it works for you.

GETTING OUT OF YOUR HEAD

You can't cross the sea merely by staring at the water.
Rabindranath Tagore

Did you think this book was all about mind games? Well, never forget you have a body. If you do, it will find a way of getting your attention – if it has to bang you on the head to do it.

◆ Everybody knows that what you do with your mind can affect your body. But do you believe it works the other way round as well?

◆ Our well-being relates to our energy levels. Movement generates serotonin and endorphins. Have you ever noticed that children laugh a lot more than adults? They also spend a lot more time running around. The two things go together. Physical activity generates 'happy' chemicals and disperses the stress-producing ones at the same time.

Some doctors even prescribe health club membership for their depressed patients now. And regular, steady, very comfortable exercise several times a week certainly works. If exercise is painful it's self defeating, you won't enjoy it, you won't keep doing it and it won't become the habit that it needs to be if you're really going to feel better.

If you think exercise is boring and gives your mind more time to worry, give yourself a double treat and listen to music – while you work out. Choose something that lifts your mood, whether it's classical, ambient, jazz or rock and roll, and if you can't find the perfect mix you can always compile your own.

GETTING INTO YOUR BODY

When we feel willing and eager, the gods join in.
Aeschylus

Body and mind are parts of the same machine and both are meant to be active. But Catch 22 is operational, as ever. When our self-esteem is low, our movements are often slow. When we are depressed our movements are clumsier and more tentative. We feel sad, so all our systems close down, we don't do much and we can get bogged down in our own despair.

Sometimes, when your mind seems set on being miserable, drastic physical intervention can change it.

Different states of mind produce different physical postures and positions. People who are depressed tend to look down a lot and move slowly. When they are treated with medication and psychotherapy, both the depression and its physical symptoms gradually disappear. A new treatment for depression which has proved remarkably successful tackles the problem from a completely different angle. It involves taking patients for a daily walk and insisting they look upwards at the sky. This is counter-instinctive for a depressed person but a lot of them found their depression starting to *lift*.

FEELGOOD FORMULA
Kitchen Timer Technique

Try these ideas out for yourself: Use a kitchen timer so that you don't get stuck in gloom.

◆ Sit down now and set the timer for two minutes. Rest your head in your hands and look at the floor. Think about something that bothers you. How easy is it to start worrying?

◆ When the timer rings, stand up with your feet shoulder-width apart, your head up and your shoulders back. Take a deep breath and look at the ceiling. See how hard it is to get depressed from that angle? You don't need to time this one. You're allowed to overrun on feeling cheerful. You probably have some time owing to you in that direction.

The kitchen timer idea is a brilliant method of controlling your worry time when you're going through a really bad patch. I know one woman who gradually eased herself off anti-depressants by allowing herself a maximum five minutes each morning and evening to worry about things. She set the timer, sat down and wrote down as many anxieties as she could think of until it rang. Then she put the worry sheet on a spike with the date on it. At the end of the week she allowed herself a ten-minute worryfest, reading through the week's lists. She knew she was getting better when she caught herself laughing at some of the items on Tuesday's list one Sunday night.

'What do you do with the lists when you've re-read them?' I asked her.

'Monday is dustbin day so I read them Sunday night and then put them in the bin' she said.

The human race has one really
effective weapon and that is laughter.
Mark Twain

Laughter is a great weapon in the battle against feeling bad. Anxiety melts like a vampire in the sun if you can laugh at one of your particularly bizarre former obsessions. Old worries are like photos of ex-girlfriends. Sometimes you wonder what on earth you could have been thinking of...

If you're having problems with making good decisions mentally, give your brain time off for bad behaviour and make some physical moves instead. It could be the kick start you need.

FEELGOOD FORMULA
Head Up and Head Down

Start from your head and work your way down to your feet with these exercises.

◆ Look up.

◆ Start with a smile. Smiling releases serotonin. Your brain can't tell the difference between a spontaneous smile and a planned one.

◆ Keep breathing, it's good for you. Breathing is one of those good things we take for granted like food, water and sunshine. Just because we *have* to do it doesn't mean that we can't do it better. Considering how important it is, most of us are very bad at breathing. The Chilling Out technique is a good way to start working on your breathing.

◆ Take up belly dancing. Moving your hips is good for your back, good for your state of mind and very good for your love life. Any kind of dancing is a mood lifter but, sadly, we live in a society where most people don't dance regularly – at least, not when they are over 25. Most people's idea of a good time seems to involve total inertia. That's not what we were designed for.

◆ Walk regularly (or cycle). Comfortable, frequent exercise releases serotonin and endorphins. You don't need to work flat out beyond your pain barrier to benefit.

◆ And relax.

FEELGOOD FORMULA
The Chilling Out Technique

Relaxation – from yoga to meditation – has great mental and physical benefits. All it requires is a few minutes peace and quiet. There are some long and elaborate methods – and people are often deterred by the thought of having to get an MBA in relaxation before they get any benefit from it. If you want quick fixes, here's one of the few that I actually recommend:

◆ Find a quiet place where you can sit undisturbed for ten to 20 minutes.

◆ Sit comfortably, back straight, face forward and both feet flat on the floor. Turn the lighting down or off. If you want all the props, light a scented candle and play some soothing music.

◆ Focus on your breathing as you notice the gentle rise and fall of your chest and stomach. Follow your breath in through your nose, right into your body and back out though your nose.

◆ Follow your breath now with more concentration. Be aware of the air streaming in through your nostrils and filling your lungs. Imagine you can see the air being drawn down deeper into your body, filling it with life.

◆ Keep your breathing at the front of your mind so that you become aware of it without thinking about it.

◆ If thoughts creep in, acknowledge them and let them go. If a thought tugs at you push it away, put it in the bin and bring your attention back to your breath.

◆ Begin to count your breaths at the end of every outward breath. Hear yourself saying the number.

◆ If you lose your place or forget the number it doesn't matter. Just start again at the beginning. The counting is simply to focus your attention on your breathing.

◆ Some days your mind is more active than others. Just accept whatever you experience, and notice the deep relaxation and peace you feel.

When you've finished give yourself a couple of minutes to get back into your life again.

RESPECTING YOURSELF

*Risk, risk anything. Care no more for the
opinion of others...Act for yourself.*
Katherine Mansfield

On my street every Sunday morning I see all these people washing their cars. They spend up to an hour doing it. I feel like saying to some of them, 'Didn't you ever hear about having a sense of priority?' The cars look great. Their owners look flabby, miserable, tired, red-eyed and hung-over. The same people who take care to put the right oil and petrol into a vehicle and have it serviced regularly, treat themselves like scrap metal. They eat junk food, they don't exercise and their idea of fun is watching rubbish on TV. Why treat your car better than you treat yourself?

We're always amazed by how amazing people are and how little they think of themselves. Most people seem to have very low self images. 'I'm not good at sport, I'm no good with figures, I can't make speeches, I'm too fat, I'm ugly...' People say that kind of thing all the time. How can they be so dismissive when their bodies are the most advanced machine ever built and their brains are the fastest and most complex computers?

Atheletes are good examples of how it's possible to co-ordinate mind and body to achieve great results. The most successful sportsmen and women are always the ones who realise that there's more to winning than practice and a healthy diet. The difference between the winners and losers is simply that the winners have learned how to use their minds to train their bodies – they are not only fit, they are also focused.

◻◻◻

FEELGOOD FORMULA
Maintenance Programme

Plan a **weekly maintenance contract** for your body and mind over the next six months.

◆ Stay in control of your day. Take one day at a time and keep your long-term goal in sight. (And if you haven't already set your long-term goal – do it now.)

◆ Every day create your own structure, with built-in support mechanisms and techniques to see you safely through the difficult patches and ensure that you get done the things that matter with the minimum of discomfort. The *Worry List* and the *Kitchen Timer* are examples of these kinds of thing.

◆ Eat at least five servings of fresh fruit and vegetables and drink at least a couple of litres of water. Minimise your intake of pre-prepared foods with chemical additives and also your use of drugs. Let the food you eat enhance your life.

◆ Include at least half an hour of exercise every day (it doesn't have to be all at once). This could be walking, gardening, cleaning, rowing, dancing, cycling, decorating or whatever happens to need doing. Keep it comfortable.

◆ Find a slot for half an hour of meditation or relaxation or yoga.

◆ Finally, find time to have fun: read or watch something that makes you laugh. Tell somebody a joke. Talk to a friend who makes you happy or do something you love to do – it could be cooking, singing or having a long, relaxing bath.

FEELGOOD FORMULA
A Good Morning

Don't just let your day happen to you. Put yourself in a good state by asking yourself the Morning Questions:

- What am I happy about in my life?
- What am I excited about in my life?
- What am I proud about in my life?
- What am I grateful of in my life?
- What am I committed to in my life?
- Who do I love? Who loves me?

FEELGOOD FORMULA
A Good Night

Set yourself up for a good night's dreaming by asking yourself the Evening Questions before you go to sleep:

- What have I given today?
- What did I learn today?
- How has today added to my quality of life?
- How is today an investment for my future?

GETTING OUT OF YOUR BOX

If it's not working – do something else!
Gloria Doris Dunham

If there was just one thing we would say to you it would be get out of your box. The trouble with living in a box is that it doesn't get more comfortable, it just gets smaller.

Change is the only constant in our lives. It's happening around us all the time. Cells are dying in our bodies all the time and millions of new ones are being made. The weather, the seasons and our lives change constantly. Yet change frightens us nearly as much as public speaking. **Why don't we admit that we are creatures of change and embrace the process?**

If you want to feel good more of your time, **break your chains** and **have more fun**. So many people seem to be asleep – and even the enlightened élite who read self-help books are looking for the authors to confirm what they already think.

◆ Do you want us to comfort you or challenge you?

◆ How do you feel now that you have nearly finished the last chapter?

◆ Are you going to make the effort to try even a few of the ideas suggested or are you going to buy yet another happy book and just keep reading for ever?

◆ What are you afraid of?

Most people admit to feeling some level of anxiety when they think about change, particularly some of the major life changes. But it can't be because we're afraid of the unknown – we can't be afraid of something we don't know about.

☐ ☐ ☐

FEELGOOD FORMULA
The Red Queen challenge

The Red Queen in *Alice in Wonderland* believed in believing several impossible things before breakfast. She was obviously one of the first lateral thinkers of the 20th century and an icon of survival for all of us.

Maybe you don't have to go as far as the Red Queen, but the idea of planning your day before breakfast and always including something you had previously thought was impossible is a sound plan. If you do that, you've effectively tamed your own phantom menace by building it into your daily structure and **making change part of your format for living**.

Feelgood Factors

◆ If you can't defeat a bad feeling with the power of thought, try physical threats.

◆ There is absolutely no chance of being happy if you aren't treating your body properly. It's like trying to stop a baby crying without first checking for hunger, wind or a wet nappy.

◆ You are unlikely to treat yourself properly if you believe deep-down that somehow you are a substandard human being. You're not. Nobody is.

◆ The most important message of this book is getting out of your box. Build risk and challenge into your daily life which is where they belong. Then you can get on with your life without constant interruption from worry and doubt.